Cruise Ships
of
THE SOLENT
PAST AND PRESENT

Andrew Cooke

Ferry
Publications

Published by:
Ferry Publications, PO Box 33, Ramsey, Isle of Man IM99 4LP
Tel: +44 (0) 1624 898445   Fax: +44 (0) 1624 898449
E-mail: ferrypubs@manx.net   Website: www.ferrypubs.co.uk

Setting the Scene

There is something about travelling by sea that holds a unique romance and timeless fascination across the globe. This is demonstrated by the crowds that line both the decks and the waterfronts when a passenger ship leaves from or arrives at a port. Having been born and raised on the Isle of Wight, I made my first ferry journey when only a few days old and the love of both the sea and sea travel is maintained forty years on. The area that makes up the Solent Region boasts an unrivalled wealth of maritime history spanning all sectors including cargo and passenger shipping, the Royal Navy, shipbuilding and of course yachting.

Why the Solent?

So, why is the Solent such a haven? We have Mother Nature to thank but where the Solent acquired its name has not been defined precisely. However, it is considered to be a bird place-name reflecting the congregations of the Solan Goose that once settled along the coastline. The first recorded use of the name Soluente dates from the early 8th century AD with the name Solentan appearing later in Saxon documentation. The present day name of Solent is not recorded in the Domesday Book. Rising sea levels escalated the Solent's river form into what it is today, the largest estuarine system on the south coast of England. The components of this system include the West and East Solent and their approaches, the Eastern harbours of Portsmouth, Langstone and Chichester, Southampton Water and other small tributary rivers such as the Rivers Beaulieu, Lymington, Medina and the Yar. The latter two are more tidal estuaries than rivers in the truest form. The sheltered nature of the Solent provides the ideal sanctuary for waterborne activity and, as a result, the region is brimming with maritime action. The approaches of the Solent are guarded to the west by the famous Needles Rocks and Lighthouse at the western tip of the Isle of Wight.

Those were the days! The imposing 1906 built Cunard Liner *Mauretania* is depicted in her element at Southampton. She held the Blue Riband for 20 years from 1907 and was painted white for a cruising role in 1930, as shown here. Withdrawal came in 1934. *(ABP Photographs at Southampton Archives)*

Cunard Line's *Queen Elizabeth* is shown here at the original Ocean Terminal in Southampton. The ship was launched by John Brown & Co. Ltd in 1938 as a consort to the *Queen Mary* and survived in transatlantic and cruising service until 1968, one year longer than the *Queen Mary*. *(FotoFlite)*

Certain liners employed tender vessels when they anchored in Ryde Roads or Cowes Roads. Sealink's Portsmouth - Ryde diesel ferry *Shanklin* was occasionally involved in this traffic but is seen here passing the 1954-built P&O liner *Arcadia* on 22nd June 1966 when on a docks cruise during the NUS strike. *(ABP Photographs at Southampton Archives)*

P&O's *Chusan* sailing down Southampton Water on a cruise on 1st July 1967. The ship entered service in 1950, ended P&O's association with services to India in 1970, undertook both liner and cruise duties and was retired and disposed of in 1973. *(John Hendy)*

Above: Union Castle Line's *Pendennis Castle* is assisted alongside at Southampton by a Red Funnel tug/tender and tug in May 1960. Built at Harland & Wolff, Belfast, in 1958 she was withdrawn in 1976 and eventually scrapped in Taiwan in 1980. (ABP *Photographs at Southampton Archives*)

Below: The powerful *United States* in Southampton Water whilst at the height of her career during August 1961. Launched in June 1951 at the Newport News Shipbuilding and Drydock Company, Virginia, she claimed the Blue Riband on her maiden transatlantic voyage in July 1952. *(Dr. Allan Ryszka-Onions)*

There has been a lighthouse on the seaward side of the jagged chalk rocks since 1859, designed by James Walker and replacing the unsuccessful cliff top example. Slightly east of this location on the mainland shore in the county of Hampshire is Hurst Spit upon which is sited Hurst Castle (built 1554) and the present day lighthouse dating from 1867. The shingle spit and restless submerged shingle banks in this area are largely responsible for the lesser variety of shipping that traverses these waters nowadays. At this point, known as the Hurst Narrows, the distance between the mainland and Isle of Wight shores is the least at just 1.2 kilometres. At the eastern end of the Solent can be found the faithful sentinel that is Nab Tower. Regularly referred to as "The Nab," this manmade structure was constructed ashore at Shoreham in West Sussex from 1918 as one of the first four submarine defence towers destined for the Dover Straits. When the First World War ended so did the urgency for these towers. The two completed examples were left to rust and in 1920 the Admiralty offered one to replace the Nab Lightship. Two tugs towed the structure out to the sand spit where it was sunk when in position. Typically the tower had a mind of its own and settled at an angle, remaining so to this day. Selsey Bill in West Sussex is located 13 kilometres north-northeast of Nab Tower and the distance by sea from this location westwards to The Needles is approximately 48 kilometres whilst the overall coastline of the Solent is around 465 kilometres in

The 1956 built and 20,263grt *Reina del Mar* is captured here leaving the Western Solent and The Needles behind her en passage from Southampton. She was built by Harland & Wolff in Belfast for liner services to South America operated by Pacific Steam Navigation Co. A change of career to a cruise vessel occurred in 1964. *(FotoFlite)*

length. Considered as a drowned valley, the Solent varies in width from 1.2 km to 8km.

One Region – Three Ports

The Solent and its inlets are unique in Britain and Europe for their hydrographical regime of four tides each day. The main driving force of the complex tides observed in the Solent arises from the tidal patterns of the English Channel. It is therefore the natural haven formed here thousands of years ago that allows the Solent to perform its invaluable role as a strategically important waterway. Three world famous maritime communities, namely the Hampshire cities of Southampton and Portsmouth plus Cowes on the Isle of Wight, have developed internationally acclaimed niches in the world of passenger liners (Southampton), the Royal Navy (Portsmouth) and yachting (Cowes). The three also share a proud history of shipbuilding and are very much linked in the present day via the cruise industry.

The Port of Southampton is located on the confluence of the River Test and River Itchen at the head of Southampton Water, a 16km long natural waterway leading in from the Solent. The characteristics of this, in conjunction with the tidal flow of the Solent, provides Southampton with an average 1.5 metre tidal range and a double high water period of around 17 hours a day in total with

little change in water level. The location and its hydrography/geography provided Southampton with the ability to become a thriving port as from the Norman Conquest of England. The first regular transatlantic steamship service commenced in 1838 plus the first foundation stone of the new docks was laid in this year. The Outer Dock (now Ocean Village Marina) opened on 29th August 1842 to serve the P&O ships *Tagus* and *Liverpool* with the Inner Dock following nine years later. The Empress Dock opened in 1890 whilst the ownership of the port passed to the London & South Western Railway in 1892. The Ocean Dock then opened in 1912 for White Star services and the New Western Docks Extension followed in 1927. Much of Southampton's port expansion could be credited to the liner trade. Indeed, almost every famous Liner has called here. Arguably the first major voyage from Southampton was made by the Pilgrims in 1620 on board the *Mayflower* and the *Speedwell*. Although this publication concentrates on the 20th-21st Century developments it is worth noting that the first liner to be converted for use as a cruise ship was the Peninsular and Oriental Steam Navigation Company's *Ceylon* in 1881. A bold move at the time considering that liner companies generally only offered their ships for cruising off season. What is now P&O Cruises was established in 1837

Built for Orient Line, P&O's *Oronsay* receives attention in Southampton's King George V dry dock in August 1967. Built in 1951 and scrapped in 1975. *(Nigel Lawrence)*

Farewell to the *Andes*. Built for Royal Mail Lines in 1939 as a liner for services to South America, the ship served as a troopship 1939-1945. A cruising career beckoned in 1959 and she is shown here leaving Southampton for the breakers on 6th May 1971. *(Dr. Allan Ryszka-Onions)*

Built by John Brown & Co. Ltd, Glasgow, in 1947, Cunard Line's *Caronia* (II) entered service in 1949. Purpose built for cruising, she earned the nickname 'Green Goddess' owing to the pale green livery. The vessel is shown here at Southampton's 101 Berth in December 1967. *(Nigel Lawrence)*

but in 1881 their terminus moved from Southampton to Tilbury. P&O returned to Southampton again in 1960 with the *Oriana* whilst the *Iberia* completed the fleet's move from Tilbury in 1969. On a local theme, the 1881 built *Rome* was also converted to a cruise ship and re-entered service in 1904 as the *Vectis*. The name of this 150 passenger vessel actually reflects that bestowed upon the Isle of Wight in Roman times.

When the 20th Century arrived Southampton was already hosting passenger ships operated by the Peninsular and Oriental Steam Navigation Company (P&O), Cunard Line, White Star Line, Royal Mail Steam Packet Company, Union Steamship Company, Hamburg-America Line, Orient Line, Nederland Line, Rotterdam Lloyd and American Line. The Union Steamship Company and Castle Mail Packet Line merged in 1900 with the first service from Southampton being operated by the *Dunottar Castle* for Union Castle Line.

In 1907 White Star Line's North Atlantic express services were transferred from Liverpool to Southampton with the first voyage from New York taken by the 1906 built *Adriatic*. Cunard Line's *Lusitania* and *Mauretania* became the world's largest liners that same year. On 25th August 1908 the American Line vessel *St. Paul* collided with HMS *Gladiator* in the western Solent off Yarmouth. Sadly, the Naval ship sank with the loss of 27 lives. Three years later the *Olympic* was involved in a collision with HMS *Hawke* as she headed outwards past Cowes. In response to Cunard's newbuilds, White Star Line's *Olympic*, *Titanic* and *Britannic* were launched in 1910, 1911 and 1914 respectively. The loss of the *Titanic* on 14th April 1912 delivered a mighty blow to her homeport and stunned the world. She lives on via her legacy like no other. The *Britannic* was originally due to be christened the *Gigantic* but the loss of her sister brought about this change. Ironically the repairs to the *Olympic* after her collision delayed completion of the *Titanic* resulting in her maiden voyage being delayed from March 1912. The size of new liners continued to increase with Hapag introducing the first of three giants, the *Imperator*, in 1911. She and her two sisters became the first liners to surpass the 50,000 gross tons barrier. That same year Cunard's *Albania* inaugurated a new service to Canada. P&O merged with British India Steam Navigation Co. in 1914 and by 1917 had a controlling share in Orient Line. The First World War saw the docks placed under Government control. As the primary port over 7,000,000 troops and around 4,000,000 tons of supplies were handled. Cunard Line switched their express liner service from Liverpool to Southampton in 1919, opened by the *Aquitania*. A prize of the First World War arrived in the form of White Star Line's 56,551grt *Majestic* in 1922. She was formerly Hamburg-America's *Bismarck*. P&O

ships graced the port again from 1925 for services to the Far East and in 1926 North German Lloyd began serving the port on their Bremen-Philadelphia line. Other companies won over by Southampton included Holland-Africa Line and French Line in 1934. Two years later the *Queen Mary* made her debut. The King George V dry dock had been completed in 1933 specifically to cater for ships such as the new Cunarder. Prior to this, smaller dry dock facilities were available plus a 288m long floating dry dock that arrived at Berth 50 in 1924 and remained until removal to Portsmouth during the Second World War. As from 1937 the port was also used by Flying Boat services. The area adjacent to what is now Town Quay was the terminal for these. Indeed the term "airport" derived from the Flying Boat era and regular services on Southampton Water ceased in September 1958.

During the Second World War, Southampton was heavily bombed and many of its facilities were destroyed or damaged. The port handled 4,300,000 troops and 3,900,000 tons of stores. After the end of the war, the Southern Railway embarked on a massive programme of modernisation and reconstruction designed to provide the accommodation and facilities worthy of the national gateway that the port was at that time. This work was continued on after nationalisation by the British Transport Commission. Passenger services resumed from Southampton using the RMS *Queen Elizabeth* from 1946 and she was joined by the RMS *Queen Mary* once again in 1947. Both had served as Troop Ships during hostilities along with a plethora of other passenger ships requisitioned, many of which also ferried home the American troops. In 1943, 25th-30th July, the *Queen Mary* carried 16,683 people, the greatest number on a floating vessel consisting of 15,740 troops and 943 crew.

The RMS *Queen Elizabeth* for example conveyed 750,000 troops and travelled 500,000 miles 1940-1946. Her war service had commenced in secret during 1940 directly from her Clyde shipyard. Mercifully plans to convert both Cunard Queens into aircraft carriers never came to fruition as their value as troopships was too great. The new facility for passenger liners, Ocean Terminal at berths 43/44, opened in 1950 and reinforced Southampton's deserved status as the U.K's premier transatlantic passenger port. The following two decades were to see UK citizens emigrate in their thousands to Australia and New Zealand aboard ships operated by the likes of Chandris, Cunard Line, Shaw Savill, P&O and British India Steam Navigation Co. By way of an example, 688,000 passengers passed through Southampton in 1955. Mayflower Terminal, the new P&O berth in western docks, was opened in 1960. In 1962 the

The *Southern Cross* entered service for Shaw Savill in 1955 for a round-the-world passenger service. She is shown here at a blustery Ocean Dock, Southampton, on 5th September 1967. Withdrawn four years later the vessel was sold for further cruising service and scrapped in 2004. *(John Hendy)*

The *Hanseatic* was built on the Clyde in 1930 as the *Empress of Japan* for Canadian Pacific Steamships and renamed *Empress of Scotland* in 1942. She passed to Hamburg Atlantic Line in 1958 for transatlantic service. Here she departs Southampton in August 1961. *(Dr. Allan Ryszka-Onions)*

The 1956 built *Reina del Mar* was the last ocean liner of the Pacific Steam Navigation Company and passed to Union Castle Line in 1964. Here she occupies Empress Dock, Southampton, in November 1967. Taiwanese breakers beckoned in 1975. *(Nigel Lawrence)*

An icon of the Liner era that survives into the 21st Century. The powerful lines of the *Queen Mary* are displayed at their best in this view of her underway in Southampton Water. The ship served Cunard Line from 1936-1967 when she then sailed to Longbeach, California for use as a floating hotel. *(FotoFlite)*

P&O's *Chitral* (2) receives maintenance in dry dock at Southampton during August 1967. Built as the *Jadotville* for Cie.Mar.Belge she quickly passed to P&O along with her sistership for service between the UK and the Far East in 1961. Scrapped 1975. *(Nigel Lawrence)*

British Transport Docks Board was set up. Alas the 1960s saw a general decline in both emigration and the liner trade. The era of jetliners was upon us and slowly eroded the dominance of the liner. By way of a welcome boost, Southampton was granted City status in 1964 due to the port's national importance. Strike action in the United Kingdom has regularly brought about the demise of flagship industries and the 1966 Seamen's Strike was no exception. Southampton was awash with passenger vessels during this time and Cunard Line alone lost £14 million in revenue. The massive disruption made it virtually impossible for the ships to regain traffic lost to air travel. Such losses were the death knoll for "Big Guns" such as the RMS *Queen Elizabeth* and RMS *Queen Mary* - withdrawn in November 1968 and October 1967 respectively. However, September 1967 saw a ship take to the water that would become a world famous icon and called Southampton her home throughout her Cunard career. The *Queen Elizabeth 2* was built to continue the historic Southampton-New York liner service but was also able to operate as a cruise ship. Built on the Clyde and named by HM The Queen, the QE2 as she was always known undertook her maiden voyage on 2nd May 1969. Having first arrived at Southampton on 8th July 1952, the powerful *United States* bowed out of service in 1969. In 2012 she survives in a state of limbo in Philadelphia, USA. The 1970s saw the end of all other liner services with another great ship, the *France* being withdrawn in October 1974 to the dismay of her namesake nation. Meanwhile ships such as the *Canberra* were switched to cruising as from 1975. Having been formed in 1900 by the merging of Union Line and the Castle Packet Company, Union Castle Line suffered an increasing drop in traffic until the inevitable happened in 1977. The *Good Hope Castle* and S.A. *Vaal* (ex *Transvaal Castle*) concluded their careers at Southampton on 26th September and 10th October respectively whilst the very last trip from South Africa, operated by the *Southampton Castle*, arrived on 24th October 1977.

The early 1980s saw the effects of battle return to Southampton when the *Canberra* and QE2 were requisitioned by the Ministry of Defence for use as troopships during the Falklands Conflict. Both were suitably converted and served vital roles before returning home work stained but safe. During this time the *Canberra* was dubbed The Great White Whale. The New Zealand ferry *Rangatira* sailed for the Falklands on 19th June 1982 as an accommodation ship. The QE2 and the *Canberra* in the meantime returned from the South Atlantic on 11th June and 11th July 1982 respectively, representing the author's most vivid childhood memories at an age of 11 years old. The *Uganda*, operated by the British India Steam

Navigation Company (part of P&O Cruises) served as a Hospital Ship at this time, using the call sign Mother Hen. She sailed into Southampton on 9th August 1982 with the Gurkha Regiment on board and actually ended her career on troop duties in the Falklands prior to lay up. The handsome Art Deco building that was Ocean Terminal was demolished in 1983 despite its status and potential role in the cruise industry. The Author visited this building just once as a lad when an exhibition was held there in 1982. This terminal's role as the prime liner berth was subsequently assumed by the 1966 built QEII Cruise Terminal at berths 38/39. This facility was opened by HM Queen Elizabeth II with the first liner to use the new facility being P&O's *Iberia*. It became the home of the QE2 when Ocean Terminal closed and remains operational in 2012 after modernisation for use by the new RMS *Queen Mary* and other such vessels from 2003.

The 1980s also heralded the rejuvenation of the passenger ship industry by way of cruising. Although names such as Orient Lines and Union Castle had been consigned to history, companies old and new explored the full potential of the

Swedish America Line's *Kungsholm* was built in 1966 by John Brown on Clydebank and is shown at Southampton on 23rd December 1974. In 1979 she became P&O's *Sea Princess* and lost the forward funnel. As the *Mona Lisa* her cruising ceased in 2010 to become a hotel ship in Oman. *(Dr. Allan Ryszka-Onions)*

cruise market that was to blossom beyond all expectations. The port of Southampton passed into the private ownership of Associated British Ports during 1982. In 1984 Princess Cruises' *Royal Princess* made her debut and was named by the Princess of Wales. The event marked the Author's first visit to Mayflower Park to witness a new arrival. This decade also heralded the era of cruise ship calls at Cowes, Isle of Wight. Historically a world centre for yachting, Cowes is located at the northern tip of the Isle of Wight and is divided by the River Medina. Boatbuilding continues whilst the bygone days also saw companies such as the British Hovercraft Corporation (East Cowes) and Samuel J. White producing a mixture of hovercraft, commercial ships and leisure craft. Depending on

Union Castle Line's *Pendennis Castle* rests at Southampton in June 1966 during the NUS Strike. Built by Harland & Wolff in 1958 she became the fastest and finest member of the Union Castle mail ship fleet. Retirement came on 14th June 1976. *(John Hendy)*

Elders & Fyffe's *Chicanoa* was built in 1958 and is shown basking in the sun at Southampton in June 1966 during the NUS Strike. In 1970 she transferred to Empressa Hondurena de Vapores S.A., Puerto Cortez and was renamed *Orica*. Sold to Greece in 1972, she was scrapped two years later. *(John Hendy)*

Built for P&O-Orient Lines in 1960 by Vickers-Armstrong of Barrow, the impressive *Oriana* passed into full P&O ownership in 1966 and served them well until 1981. A career in static use then saw her survive until 2005. Here the ship passes Calshot outward bound in November 1979. *(Dr. Allan Ryszka-Onions)*

Sitmar's *Fairwind* and *Fairland* laid up at Southampton's Berth 101 in November 1968. The *Fairwind* began life as Cunard's *Sylvania* in 1957 and sistership *Fairland* was built as Cunard's *Carinthia*. Both passed to Princess Cruises and were later scrapped in 2004 and 2005 respectively. *(Nigel Lawrence)*

Having returned to Southampton from her war duties in the Falkland Islands on 11th June 1982 the *Queen Elizabeth 2* was restored to full passenger service at the UK Government's expense. She also received the unpopular grey hull, a look that thankfully only lasted a few months. *(FotoFlite)*

Pictured at Calshot in 1993, the *Achille Lauro* was delivered in 1947 as the *Willem Ruys* and sold to Lauro Lines in 1964 to be named after her Italian owner. The liner/cruise ship became world famous in 1985 when hijacked by terrorists but caught fire and sank in 1994. *(Dr. Allan Ryszka-Onions)*

The *S. A. Vaal* at Southampton during the Seaman's Strike in June 1966. Launched in 1961 as the *Transvaal Castle*, the ship was transferred to the South African Marine Corp (UK) in 1966 and renamed. Sold to Carnival Cruises in 1977, her days ended as the *Big Red Boat III*. *(John Kennedy)*

Cunard Line's *Caronia* is depicted at Southampton's Queen Elizabeth II Cruise Terminal in June 2003. The ship was built as the *Vistafjord* in 1973, passed to Cunard in 1983, renamed in 1999 and was sold to Saga Cruises in 2004 to become their *Saga Ruby*. *(Andrew Cooke)*

Built in 1960 as the *Bore*, this vessel was renamed *Kristina Regina* in 1988 after conversion from ferry to cruise ship by Finnish operator Kristina Cruises. Now a Hotel Ship in Turku, she visited the Solent for the D-Day 50th Anniversary Fleet Review on 5th June 1994 as shown here. *(Andrew Cooke)*

Premier Cruises' *Rembrandt* was built as Holland America Lines' *Rotterdam* in 1959 before taking this name in October 1997. The ship is depicted at Southampton's Berth 38/39 a few months later. Her classic profile lives on in 2012 as the floating hotel *Rotterdam* in her namesake port. *(Andrew Cooke)*

Phoenix Reisen's *Albatros* is shown at Southampton in May 1996 awaiting repairs after grounding off the Isles of Scilly just days earlier. Built in 1957 as the *Sylvania* she later became the *Fairwind* (see page 13) and survived until 2004 when scrapped at Alang, India. *(Andrew Cooke)*

P&O Cruises' *Sea Princess* soaks up the summer sun at Southampton's Mayflower Cruise Terminal in August 1993. Built in 1966 as the *Kungsholm*, she passed to P&O and lost a funnel in 1978 (see page 11) and finished her P&O career as the *Victoria* in 2002. *(Andrew Cooke)*

The unmistakable lines of the *Saga Rose* are displayed here as she catches the evening sunshine off Cowes in 2009 whilst outbound from Southampton. She was launched in 1964 for Norwegian America Line as the *Sagafjord* and later passed to Saga from Cunard Line in 1997. *(John Hendy)*

Celebrity Cruises' *Celebrity Constellation* was the fourth of a quartet of gas turbine powered Millennium Class ships built at St. Nazaire in France. She returned to Southampton for a series of cruises from September 2012 and is shown here off Cowes, Isle of Wight. *(Andrew Cooke)*

In 2011 Swan Hellenic Cruises commenced turnaround cruises from Portsmouth using their 1996 built *Minerva*. The vessel was created using the partially completed hull of a Soviet-ordered research ship. Here she is shown passing Portsmouth's Spinnaker Tower whilst outward bound. *(Andrew Cooke)*

Italian operator MSC Cruises transferred its seasonal UK operations from Dover to Southampton in 2011. To raise the company's profile prior to this the brand new *MSC Magnifica* was showcased at the Hampshire port in February 2010 and is shown here inward bound after delivery. *(Andrew Cooke)*

Yellow Peril and Yellow Funnel: The IKEA branded Red Funnel ferry *Red Osprey* approaches Cowes as P&O Cruises' 1995 built *Oriana* also leaves Southampton in her wake en route to warmer climes during the Summer of 2009. *(Andrew Cooke)*

An unusual view of the *Thomson Celebration* berthed at Southampton's City Cruise Terminal in May 2005 as viewed from an aircraft leaving Southampton Airport. The ship was built as Holland America Line's *Noordam* in 1984 and chartered to Thomson Cruises in 2004 after refit in Falmouth. *(Nigel Lawrence)*

size and weather conditions, visiting cruise ships generally anchor in one of three locations; the Cowes side of the Solent's main shipping channel (an area known as Cowes Triangle), north of the main channel in an area known as the Front Line or in the Salt Mead Anchorage in Thorness Bay when more shelter is required. Since 2006 cruise ship tenders have been able to use the Trinity Landing pontoon on Cowes Parade. Smaller ships, from the fleets of operators such as Hapag Lloyd, frequent Cowes with one of the largest visitors being the 28,891gt *Mona Lisa* in 2010. Sadly the weather that day prevented the ship from anchoring and she continued to her next call in France. There are generally no more than half a dozen visitors per annum and, unlike Southampton and Portsmouth, no turnaround cruises are handled here.

The 1990s further reignited the cruise industry and the first major event at the port was the arrival of P&O's flagship *Oriana* from the Meyer Werft Shipyard in Germany during April 1995 – the port's first new ocean going passenger vessel since the QE2. She was named by HM The Queen. In 1996 the navigation channel was deepened in readiness for larger ships and on 30th September 1997 the *Canberra* concluded her revenue earning career, being welcomed home by a flotilla of vessels reminiscent of her 1982 homecoming and "escorted" by HMS *Cornwall*. Both this event and her Falklands homecoming saw her shrouded in mist for much of the inbound journey from Nab Tower. The following day the grand old lady moved to berth 38/39 to make way for the *Oriana* and de-storing commenced in earnest. The vessel was denied a much deserved big send-off when she slipped quietly away at 21.00hrs on 10th October with lights ablaze bound for the Breakers in Pakistan. She was run aground on the beach at Gadani on 31st October 1997 – end of an era. Ironically, her 1960 built former consort *Oriana* outlived *Canberra* by eight years. The last English built liner, and final remnant of Orient Line, was scrapped in 2005 after a long period of preservation in Dalian, China. The remainder of the 1990s also witnessed visits by Festival Cruise Line's *Mistral*, Disney Cruises' *Disney Wonder* and P&O Cruises' *Arcadia* to name but three. The latter was a stop-gap measure until the delivery of the next new build. Meanwhile Portsmouth tentatively dipped its toe into the world of cruising in April 1993 when P&O Portsmouth introduced the 37,583gt cruiseferry *Pride of Bilbao* that linked Portsmouth with Bilbao in Spain for the next 17 years. Minicruises proved very popular with Brittany Ferries and AT Ferries then also offering such sailings although the latter was short-lived. Better was to come of course.

New Millennium – New Era

The early to mid-part of the 20th Century is often referred to as the heyday of passenger shipping but the quantity and size of such ships has grown beyond all expectations since the dawn of the new millennium. P&O Cruises' *Aurora*, a refined version of the 1995 built *Oriana*, arrived in 2000. A year later saw visits by the new *Golden Princess* (Princess Cruises), *Adventure of the Seas* (Royal Caribbean International) and *Norwegian Sun* (Norwegian Cruise Lines) whilst Fred Olsen's third ship, the *Braemar*, arrived on the scene. During 2001 Portsmouth also embarked upon its full scale entry into the cruise market. Besides its world famous history as a naval port and cross-Solent ferry/deep sea commercial trade, passenger shipping first came to the port in 1976 when Portsmouth International Port opened for cross-channel ferry traffic to France. Successful dialogue with Portsmouth Naval Base had meant that naval berths could be utilised for visiting cruise ships.

May 2003 saw the "White Sisters" *Adonia* and *Oceana* transferred to Southampton from the Princess Cruises fleet. These were formerly the *Sea Princess* and *Ocean Princess*. Both were re-named for P&O service by The Princess Royal and her Daughter Zara Phillips with the duo later sailing in tandem down Southampton Water for their official debut. The new City Cruise Terminal (Berth 101) was completed and opened in 2003 (rebuilt 2007) primarily for use by Fred Olsen Cruises, Saga Cruises, Royal Caribbean and Thomson Cruises. Surely the biggest event of the decade now known as the "Noughties" took place on 26th December 2003 when Cunard Line's spectacular new liner *Queen Mary 2* arrived from her builders in St. Nazaire, France. After much celebration her maiden voyage departed on 12th January 2004 and Cunard once again had two Queens based at the home of cruising. Royal Caribbean International's (RCI) *Jewel of the Seas* was christened at Southampton in 2004 with fleet mate *Legend of the Seas* operating RCI cruises from here in 2005. Between 2005 and 2007 the King George V dry dock, a Grade II Listed Structure, was gradually run down and closed – the last of seven such amenities that once graced the port. One of the last cruise ships to use the dock was the *Adonia* when she was returned to her former identity of *Sea Princess*. From then on the closest dry dock of any size was at A&P Appledore's Falmouth yard in Cornwall but many

Opposite page: **Welcome Home! One of Southampton's Svitzer tugs, the *Svitzer Sarah*, welcomes the *Queen Mary 2* home in a celebratory manner on the morning of 5th June 2012 when all three Cunarders sailed in at daybreak to celebrate the Diamond Jubilee of Her Majesty Queen Elizabeth II.** (*Andrew Cooke*)

Southampton based vessels visit Bremerhaven and Hamburg to name but two. The evolution of the cruise ship from the 1980s to the 2000s was quite astounding. Another record breaker to grace Southampton was RCI's 154,407gt *Freedom of the Seas*. The world's largest in terms of tonnage; she arrived from her builders, Aker Finnyards of Turku in Finland, at the end of April 2006 for a showcase event prior to continuing for New York. In contrast, May of this year also saw Portsmouth welcome its largest cruise ship to date, the 28,518gt *Albatros*. In December 2006 another of Norwegian Cruises Line's new class of Freestyle Cruising ships, the 93,530gt *Norwegian Pearl*, was showcased at Southampton. Two years later sister Jewel Class ship *Norwegian Jade* (formerly *Pride of Hawaii*) operated from the port for two seasons. During April 2007 RCI's second record breaker, the 154,407gt *Liberty of the Seas* arrived from her builders in Finland whilst en route to the USA. Here she rendezvoused with the slightly smaller 138,270gt *Navigator of the Seas*, having arrived for her 2007 season, and the pair staged a "kiss" as the *Liberty of the Seas* departed. The Vista Class build originally intended to be Cunard Line's third Queen was completed by Fincantieri in Italy as P&O's *Arcadia* in 2005 (replacing the short lived namesake that was formerly the 1989 built *Star Princess*). However, in December 2007 the new 90,049gt *Queen Victoria* finally arrived at her new home. Another notable visitor to Portsmouth in 2007 was Saga Cruises' 24,002gt *Saga Rose* upon completion of her 44th world cruise.

The year 2008 brought the arrival of two more milestone vessels. On 6th April the largest ship built for the UK cruise industry, P&O Cruises' 116,017gt *Ventura*, sailed up Southampton Water in an unseasonal blizzard. Later that month the biggest cruise ship to be based in the UK so far arrived. With a gross tonnage of 154,407, making her the world's largest cruise vessel at that time, the *Independence of the Seas* commenced a programme of seasonal, then year-round cruises in May 2008 that became seasonal again as from winter 2012. In June 2008 Holland America Line's (HAL) shiny new *Eurodam*, an 86,273gt Signature Class ship, visited the port to showcase the HAL product. No ship can last in service forever, no matter how famous, and 11th November 2008 saw Southampton say a sad yet celebratory farewell to Cunard Line's QE2 as she set sail on her final voyage to Dubai. It was an end of an era. Six months earlier she had also taken part in the City's first Cunard Line Three Queens event. The new, but by no means as grand, Ocean Terminal officially opened at Berth 46 adjacent to the site of the old one in May 2009. The first ship to use it was the *Oceana* but the official event saw the *Ventura* present. Celebrity Cruises' second Solstice

Class ship, *Celebrity Equinox*, visited in July 2009 on her delivery voyage from Meyer Werft and, by way of things to come, offered two cruises from the City Cruise Terminal. Saga Cruises' *Saga Rose* and Fred Olsen Cruises' *Black Prince* both concluded their mainstream careers in this year prior to sailing for eventual scrap and Venezuela respectively. A gigantic event in every way took place in November 2009 when the 225,282gt *Oasis of the Seas* ventured into Charlie Anchorage in the Western Solent en route from her builders in Finland to Fort Lauderdale. Taking the crown as the world's largest cruise ship this floating goliath disembarked shipyard workers onto Blue Funnel's *Ashleigh-R* for transfer to Southampton prior to continuing on her way. The Author was present on-board one of the local "Jenny" boats during a hastily arranged sightseeing trip. It is said that the *Oasis of the Seas* did not berth in Southampton for this purpose as RCI wanted her first port arrival to be Fort Lauderdale. Alas the hoped for visit of sistership *Allure of the Seas* never materialised. The following year was a bumper issue that began with the February arrival of the brand new 95,128gt *MSC Magnifica* for a two night event. April 10th saw the 115,055 *Azura* arrive for P&O Cruises followed by the 121,878gt *Celebrity Eclipse*. This vessel then made a mercy dash to Bilbao in the middle of her celebrations to collect a consignment of passengers stranded in Spain as a result of the now infamous volcanic ash cloud originating in Iceland that grounded passenger aircraft across much of Europe. The use of the ship was a Public Relations Manager's dream. The *Celebrity Eclipse* was then named at City Cruise Terminal by way of a ceremony conducted in the on board theatre and a "live" camera link to a bottle positioned on the ship's forward funnel. However the big screen footage was pre-recorded earlier in the day as it showed blue skies as the bottle smashed when those of us gathered in front of the ship in Mayflower Park were under cloudy skies! Norwegian Cruise Line's new 155,873gt *Norwegian Epic* graced Southampton in June 2010, arriving with a propulsion problem and sailing two days later after her introduction to the UK market with a sell-out transatlantic voyage to New York. Four months later the "replacement" for the QE2 arrived in the form of the 90,901gt *Queen Elizabeth*, another of the ubiquitous Vista Class of vessel built by Italian Shipyard Fincantieri.

Having achieved a six fold increase in cruise calls since becoming a cruise port in 2001, Portsmouth celebrated its tenth anniversary in 2011. A state of the art new passenger terminal opened over the Easter of that year as part of a £16.5 million investment in new facilities. The first vessel to use the new terminal was the 16,144gt *Athena*. The ferry berths had been utilised by cruise

Cunard Line's 2007 built *Queen Victoria* sails from Southampton's Ocean Terminal in July 2012. Red Funnel's 1996 built *Red Eagle*, with funnel adorned with a Union Jack for that summer's events, had waited for her to clear the docks prior to continuing her journey from East Cowes. *(Andrew Cooke)*

The Hythe Ferry *Hotspur IV* has seen many a cruise ship and liner come and go since she entered service in 1946. Freshly adorned in a new colour scheme in July 2012 she is passed at Hythe Pier by the splendid *Oriana*, the first superliner built for the UK market in 1995. *(Andrew Cooke)*

History was made in November 2009 when Royal Caribbean's brand new *Oasis of the Seas* visited the eastern Solent to disembark workers whilst on her delivery voyage from Finland to Miami. She was the world's largest cruise ship and the largest such vessel to visit the Solent. *(Andrew Cooke)*

A busy scene in Southampton's Western Docks. The *Queen Mary 2* is at the Mayflower Cruise Terminal whilst Fred. Olsen Cruises' *Braemar* is at the City Cruise Terminal. The latter was built in 1993 as the *Crown Dynasty*, sold to Fred. Olsen in 2001 and stretched in 2008. *(Andrew Cooke)*

The third of Celebrity Cruises' Solstice Class ships, the *Celebrity Eclipse*, was based in Southampton from new in April 2010. Here she is shown returning from Bilbao in Spain having collected holidaymakers stranded by the Icelandic ash cloud that grounded flights in Europe. *(Andrew Cooke)*

The *Saga Pearl II* joined Saga Cruises in 2010 and is shown here at City Cruise Terminal in October 2010. The ship was built in 1981, previously carried the name *Astoria* and was renamed *Quest for Adventure* in May 2012. Astern of her is P&O Cruises' 2008 built *Ventura*. *(Andrew Cooke)*

visitors since the decrease in ferry operations in 2004/2005 and then Berth 2 was extended by 50 metres to accommodate one large or two smaller ships. The first vessel to use this after completion was the 22,080gt *Marco Polo* on 31st May 2012. Operators using the port now included Swan Hellenic, Voyages of Discovery Cruises, Hebridean Island Cruises, Fred Olsen Cruises Lines, Sea Cloud Cruises, Hapag Lloyd and Hurtigruten Cruises. With Portsmouth undertaking turnaround cruises for the likes of the 1971 built *Discovery*, the *Minerva* and *Hebridean Princess*, nearby Southampton welcomed the *Adonia* on 20th May 2011. The 30,277gt vessel became P&O Cruises' smallest ship and effectively replaced the *Artemis* (built as the *Royal Princess*) that was withdrawn the previous month and became Phoenix Reisen's *Artania*. By coincidence the *Adonia*'s previous identity was also the *Royal Princess* and began life in 2001 as the *R Eight*. Alas towards the end of 2011 the Cunard trio's port of registry was switched from Southampton to Hamilton to permit weddings at sea – thus ending 171 years of Cunard ships on the British registry.

The year in which this book was completed, 2012, was quite a time for events at Southampton. The Centenary of the *Titanic* departing Southampton was commemorated on 10th April with the help of resident excursion steamship *Shieldhall* that had received a black hull for the occasion plus other vessels including the preserved tug/tender *Calshot*. Then, during the Diamond Jubilee Celebrations for H.M The Queen the three

Cunarders sailed into Southampton together for the first time on 5th June. The QM2 lead the *Queen Victoria* and *Queen Elizabeth* home before, after some manoeuvring, the three ships achieved a "three bows" meeting east of Mayflower Park. The *Queen Elizabeth* was bows west at City Cruise Terminal, the *Queen Victoria* went alongside bow to bow with her sister whilst the QM2 sailed down past to complete the scene accompanied by much cheering, waving and whistle blowing. The *Queen Victoria* then moved astern to the Mayflower Terminal with the QM2 proceeding to Ocean Terminal. The weather worsened throughout the day causing the cancellation of the flypasts by the Red Arrows. But the events on board each ship went ahead including numerous VIPs such as Princess Anne, Esther Rantzen and Darcy Bussell. That evening the *Queen Victoria* and QM2 moved to a close proximity with the *Queen Elizabeth* for celebratory fireworks at 22.20 prior to all three ships departing. Four weeks later came P&O Cruises' Grand Event to celebrate their 175th Anniversary. In an unprecedented move all seven ships of the fleet were in port on that day. The *Adonia* and *Oceana* shared the QEII Terminal whilst the *Azura* occupied Ocean Terminal and the *Oriana*, *Aurora*, *Arcadia* and *Ventura* sat line astern between City Cruise Terminal and Mayflower Cruise Terminal in Western Docks. Some 70,000 passengers passed through the port that day, again the weather deteriorated into gloom and rain but the atmosphere was incredible as the sailaway unfolded. The *Adonia* commenced the departure

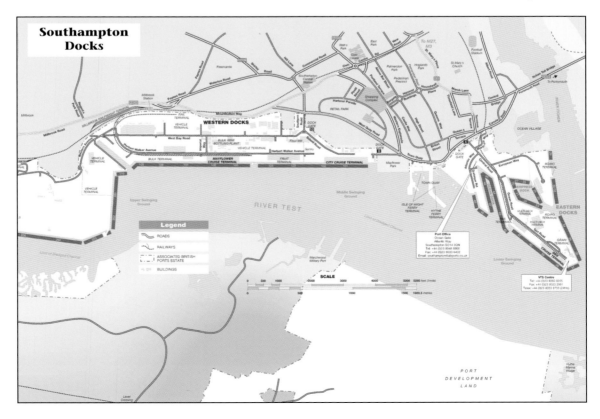

Silversea Cruises' vessels are regular visitors to Southampton and in 2012 the 2001 built *Silver Whisper* offered a programme of cruises from the port. The 388 passenger capacity ship was built by T. Mariotti SpA, Genoa, Italy. Here she sails down Southampton Water in May 2012. *(Andrew Cooke)*

The *Balmoral* passes Calshot with another cruise during Summer 2011. She began life as the *Crown Odyssey* in 1988 for Royal Cruise Line and became the *Norwegian Crown* in 1996. Sold to Fred. Olsen Cruises in 2006, the ship was lengthened and entered service in 2008. *(Andrew Cooke)*

sequence by proceeding to the Western Swinging Ground and, after turning, was followed by each of her fleet mates in turn amidst a cacophony of whistle blowing from the seven ships and the flotilla of spectator craft. One by one the *Ventura*, *Arcadia*, *Aurora*, *Oriana*, *Azura* and *Oceana* each slipped their moorings to follow the *Adonia* outward down Southampton Water. A pyrotechnic display was given to each ship as they passed east of Dock Head. Once in the Eastern Solent the line split into two columns to pass either side of the Trinity House Vessel (THV) *Patricia* for a Royal Review by The Princess Royal. The fleet then went their separate ways once beyond Nab Tower having made a fantastic sight despite the murky weather. Just over a week later on 13th July the three Cunarders were again reunited in Southampton with scheduled turnaround calls. Considering the abysmal summer weather up to that time the sun did manage to shine as the *Queen Elizabeth* sailed from Mayflower Terminal and proceeded outbound with much whistle blowing as she was followed by the *Queen Victoria* at Ocean Terminal and they both sailed past the QM2 at the QEII Terminal. The two "Vista Sisters" then slowed to await the departure of their big sister which then did her best to catch up with the formation. This was the first occasion that the trio had sailed in formation away from Southampton in daylight hours. The London 2012 Olympic Torch Relay ensemble visited the Isle of Wight on 14th July and was conveyed back to Southampton aboard the Red Funnel Raptor Class car ferry *Red Eagle*. Escorted by HMS *Exploit*, *Red Jet 4* and *Red Jet 5* plus a flotilla of other craft the ferry met the departing *Independence of the Seas*, *Azura* and *Oriana*. There was much whistle blowing – in the rain again – with cruise passengers lining the decks to see the vessels pass them.

Plans for a fifth cruise terminal between the Mayflower and City Cruise facilities were put on hold in July 2012 following the uncertainty of any potential impact of Liverpool's attempts to establish itself as a turnaround cruise port. That said, it can only be a matter of time before further expansion at Southampton is needed to maintain its majority share of the UK cruise market, which has experienced a 400% growth since 2000. ABP figures also show that the cruising industry at the Port of Southampton generates over £300m a year for the local economy. In 2000 there were 147 calls that generated 330,000 passengers and ten years later the cruise calls had escalated to 301 resulting in around 1,182,000 passengers through the port. In 2011 there was a further 19.3 per cent rise in cruise passenger numbers generated by a further 63 cruise calls. Between 2013 and 2015 the Solent can

also look forward to welcoming the new 39,500gt *Europa 2* of Hapag Lloyd, the 144,017gt Norwegian Cruise Line ship *Norwegian Breakaway*, the 141,000gt *Royal Princess* of Princess Cruises plus the as yet un-named £340m and 141,000gt newbuild for P&O Cruises – to name but four. Despite well publicised financial woes around the world the cruise industry is riding a crest of a wave and it is full steam ahead for the future.

Among the ranks of classic passenger ships to have served the Solent and Southampton over the years, a handful of individuals have gained eternal popularity across the globe and will never be forgotten. Two such ships, the *Canberra* and the *France*, are very different in design but were both built for liner services prior to being transformed for cruising roles.

The *CANBERRA*

The post war years brought about a new era of emigration from Great Britain with the bulk of those wishing to travel to pastures new setting their sights on Australia and New Zealand. As the Jet Age began to unfold, P&O placed an order for a new ship to meet the demand on their Australia service. On 23rd September 1957, the first keel sections of yard no. 1621 were pieced together at Belfast's Harland & Wolff shipyard. After much deliberation it was not until March 1958 that the new ship's name was revealed to the world – and the *Canberra* was born. Christened after an aboriginal word meaning 'meeting place by the water,' the ship also shared her name with Australia's capital city. The largest ship to be built at Harland & Wolff since White Star Line's *Britannic* of 1914; the *Canberra* was launched on 16th March 1960. Dame Pattie Menzies, wife of the Australian Prime Minister, took the honour of christening the new ship. A large bottle of Australian wine was used for the ceremony in favour of the traditional champagne. After fitting out had been completed the ship embarked on sea trials in Belfast Lough on 29th April 1961. The vessel's modern profile set her apart from many other ships of that time and, because her machinery had been positioned aft to increase space for passenger areas, the funnels were also located towards the stern. The iconic profile of these funnels lives on through the design of the 1995 built *Oriana*. The *Canberra*'s fleet mate was to be Orient Line's new *Oriana*, also under construction at that time. The two operators had shared the Australia-UK mail contract and merged operations soon after their respective new builds had taken to the water to create P&O-Orient Lines in 1960. The £17 million and twin-screw *Canberra* boasted a tonnage of 45,270grt when built and this

On 3rd July 2012 P&O Cruises celebrated their 175th Anniversary with a Grand Event at Southampton involving all seven ships. Here the *Adonia* leads the *Ventura*, *Arcadia*, *Aurora*, *Oriana*, *Azura* and *Oceana* away from Southampton through the eastern Solent. *(P&O Cruises)*

On two occasions in 2012 Cunard Line's three ships were in Southampton together. The second event was 13th July and here the *Queen Elizabeth* leads the *Queen Victoria* past the *Queen Mary 2* prior to waiting for the latter to join the procession down Southampton Water. *(Andrew Cooke)*

was revised to 49,073grt in the latter part of her career for the cruise trade. Her overall length was 249.9 metres with a beam of 31.2 metres and draught of 9.97 metres. Propulsion was provided by two British Thompson Houston (AEI) synchronous three-phase, 6,000 volt air-cooled electric motors providing 63,000 kW with power supplied by two 32,200 kW steam turbine driven alternators. Indeed the *Canberra's* steam turbo-electric units were the most powerful of their type ever installed in a passenger ship. The maximum speed achieved during trials was 29.27 knots with the service speed being set at 27.5 knots. During trials in May 1961 her bows lifted almost out of the water at speed so an appropriate quantity of concrete was added to the forward compartments as ballast. When new her two-class accommodation catered for 548 First-class and 1,690 Tourist class passengers plus 960 officers and crew. The First-class area occupied the forward section and Tourist class was located in the remainder of the passenger accommodation. The *Canberra's* appearance was also enhanced by the ship's lifeboats being placed in recesses in the hull closer to the waterline, something adopted by some of today's cruise ship designs. The *Canberra* sailed to Southampton from Belfast on 28th April 1961 and commenced her maiden 42,000 mile return voyage to Australia via Suez on 2nd June that year. Initial problems with her steam condensers and other machinery plagued performance until all issues were ironed out. The late 1960s/early 1970s saw the emigration to Australia stagnate whilst commercial airliners were fast taking over the trade. P&O decided to send the *Canberra* to New York to offer Caribbean cruises. However, this venture failed and P&O announced that the ship would be sent to the ship breakers at the end of the 1973 season. Fortunately an increase in the UK cruise market saw the vessel retained and converted to a new life as a pure cruise ship based at Southampton. As a single class ship her capacity was reduced to 1,700 passengers whilst the service speed was also adjusted to 23.50 knots. The *Canberra* remained hugely popular throughout her career but her finest hour came in 1982 when called upon to serve her country. On 2nd April 1982, Argentina invaded the Falkland Islands, which initiated the Falklands War. At this time the *Canberra* was on a Mediterranean cruise when the Captain was advised that the Ministry of Defence had requisitioned the vessel for use as a troopship. The *Canberra* steamed home to Southampton where she was quickly refitted, sailing on 9th April for the South Atlantic. This duty earned her the nickname "Great White Whale" as she transported the Parachute Regiment and Royal Marines to the Falklands. Unlike fellow troopship the *Queen Elizabeth 2*, the *Canberra* found herself at the centre

of the conflict in San Carlos Water on 21st May whilst the landings took place. She then embarked 3,000 troops from the QE2 at South Georgia and returned to the war zone. When the conflict had ended the ship repatriated 4,000 captured Argentine soldiers, landing them at Puerto Madryn, before returning to Southampton to a rapturous welcome on 11th July. After much tender loving care the ship resumed her cruising career on 11th September 1982. With the arrival of the new *Oriana* in April 1995 the *Canberra's* days were sadly numbered. The following year her withdrawal was announced and on 30th September 1997 this fine ship arrived home for the final time to a fantastic welcome. She was escorted by *HMS Cornwall* and a large flotilla of vessels plus there were flypasts by the Red Arrows and a Canberra Bomber. Premier Cruise Line reportedly made a bid for the grand old lady but P&O had already decided that they did not want the *Canberra* to operate under a different flag. Indeed, on 10th October came the announcement that the ship had been sold to ship breakers in Pakistan. She sailed from Southampton at 21.00 that night and beached herself where ships go to die at Gadani 21 days later. The ship put up a fight and was not finally demolished until the end of 1998.

The *FRANCE*

Following the loss of the *Normandie* in New York Harbour in 1942, the *Ile de France* became the only transatlantic liner serving Compagnie Générale Transatlantique (CGT – also known as French Line)

Following her capture during World War 2, the German liner *Europa* was subsequently passed to CGT where she gained the appropriate name of *Liberte*. The two vessels maintained liner services through the 1950s but, following the introduction of Cunard's *Queen Elizabeth* in 1946, the French operator strived to outshine its competitor. A brand new $80 million liner was ordered from the shipyard Chantiers d'Atlantique at St Nazaire, France with construction beginning on 7th September 1957. This icon of passenger shipping was launched on 11th May 1960 by Madame Yvonne de Gaulle, wife of the President of France and the blessing was undertaken by the Bishop of Nantes. With a gross tonnage of 66,348 the graceful new ship claimed the title of the longest passenger ship ever built – an accolade that she held on to until the *Queen Mary 2* was built at the same yard over forty years later. The stylish *France* was the third CGT ship to carry that name and also the last liner to operate under the French flag. She was created as an ocean-going showcase for the nation, the hull was fully welded to save weight and two sets of stabilisers were installed. Sea trials commenced on 19th November 1961 and the *France* sailed on her first voyage, a cruise to the

The *Canberra* is given a grand send off as she makes her way towards the Solent on her farewell cruise in September 1997. The tug with the enthusiastic water display is Red Funnel Towage's *Redbridge*. Red Funnel's Southampton based tug operation was sold in 2002. *(Andrew Cooke)*

P&O Cruises' unforgettable *Canberra* began her career in 1961 and here she is shown having concluded her farewell cruise at Southampton's Mayflower Terminal on 30th September 1997. Also present is Blue Funnel's *Poole Scene* – the former Gosport Ferry *Southsea Queen*. *(Andrew Cooke)*

The magnificent Liner *France* arrives at Southampton on 20th January 1962 when brand new on a shakedown cruise bound for Tenerife. Her maiden Le Havre-New York crossing took place in early February 1962. Withdrawal came just twelve years later. *(ABP Photographs at Southampton Archives)*

From 1979 the Liner *France* became the cruise liner *Norway* until withdrawal from the Norwegian Cruise Lines fleet in 2004. Here the *Norway* is shown in her less graceful rebuilt form at the Queen Elizabeth II Terminal at Southampton. *(Andrew Cooke)*

Canary Islands, on 19th January 1962. The maiden transatlantic crossing departed from Le Havre to New York on 3rd February 1962. Sea trials had produced a top speed of 35.21 knots with the service speed being 31 knots. The *France* was designed and built with speed and comfort in mind, and used the most advanced technology of the time for the propulsion system and other power generating machinery. Fuel costs were also an added factor. The engines consisted of eight high-pressure, super-heating boilers, weighing a total of 8,000 tons and operating at 500 degrees Celsius. These delivered 175,000 horsepower whilst the fuel consumption amounted to 750 tonnes of oil in a 24 hour period. The geared CEM-Parsons turbine units that powered the four propellers were divided into two fore and aft groups, as was the electrical generating equipment. The vessel had a beam of 33.70 metres, a draught of 10.80 metres and a deadweight of 13,961 tons. The *France* was also built with a unique double bottom that enabled her to carry 8,000 tons of fuel - enough for a Le Havre-New York-Le Havre round trip. Passenger capacity was 2,044 (407 in First class and 1,637 in Tourist class) with each area even having its own swimming pool. Between 13th-26th July 1967 the *France* was at the Ile Notre-Dame in Montreal, acting as a secondary French pavilion at the 1967 World's Fair, Expo 67.

The ship's cruises also proved popular, with her first world cruise taking place in 1972. Operating costs spiralled in the early 1970s and the French Government decided to divert the additional subsidies required to the Concorde project instead. Without these funds, the French Line could not operate, and with a press release issued in 1974 it was announced that the *France* would be withdrawn from service on 25th October that year. This declaration was deemed a national disgrace. By way of objection the crew decided to strike upon returning to Le Havre from New York on 12th September 1974. The ship was anchored in the entrance to the port, thereby blocking all incoming and outgoing traffic. The 1,200 passengers aboard had to go ashore by tender. The striker's mission failed and their actions effectively caused a premature end to the *France* as she did not sail again. She was occupied for over a month at the end of a career that saw her complete 377 crossings and 93 cruises. With no desire to sell the ship she remained laid up for four years. Eventually a sale was completed in 1979 to Knut Kloster, the owner of what became Norwegian Cruise Line, for $18 million for conversion into the world's largest cruise ship. During her refit, two propellers and four boilers were removed, reducing the ship's top speed to a maximum of 25 knots.

The *France* was renamed *Norway* and moved to the Lloyd Werft shipyard in Germany, where she received an $80,000,000 refit. Registered in Oslo, the ship was officially re-christened on 3rd May 1980 by King Olav V. Alas the liner's sleek lines were disfigured in 1990 by the addition of two decks atop her superstructure to accommodate 135 new suites and luxury cabins. This increased her passenger capacity to 2,565 and her gross tonnage to 76,049 tons. For her cruising role the ship also had two large tenders installed on her foredeck, complete with their own lifting gantries. Classed as ships themselves, and named the *Little Norway 1* and *Little Norway 2*, they gave the *Norway* the distinction of being the only ship to carry two ships as a matter of routine. The refit at Southampton in 1996 did little to improve the ravages of age on this ever popular ship. Alas mechanical issues became more frequent and the *Norway's* status began to slide. Her final calls at Le Havre and Southampton came in 2001 and on 25th May 2003, after a routine arrival at Miami, the *Norway* was seriously damaged by a boiler explosion. Sadly this killed eight crew members, and injured seventeen, as superheated steam engulfed the boiler room and blew into crew quarters above through ruptured decking. None of the passengers were injured. The probable cause was given as poor boiler operation and maintenance. On 27th June 2003 the stricken *Norway* was towed from Miami bound for Bremerhaven and in March of the following year it was announced that she would never sail again. Her asbestos content then caused a long and complicated process to permit demolition. The ship was towed from Germany on 23rd May 2005 bound for Port Kelang in Malaysia. Following sale in April 2006 the once proud liner was renamed *Blue Lady* and, after a further sale and more legal wrangling concerning her asbestos, found herself off the coast of India four months later. A Court ruling finally permitted the scrapping of the ship at Alang in September 2007 and by the end of 2008 she was no more.

The graceful and unique lines of the *France* are captured in this painting of the liner arriving at New York from Le Havre and Southampton at the beginning of her career. Strike action ahead of her withdrawal in 1974 denied the ship the send-off that she deserved. *(Painting by Robert Lloyd, by kind courtesy of Miles Cowsill)*

P&O Cruises' first Grand Class ship, the *Ventura*, was built by Fincantieri's Monfalcone Yard in Italy and made her debut at Southampton on 6th April 2008. Incredibly she sailed up Southampton Water in a snow storm! Here she leaves the Ocean Terminal in May 2012. *(Andrew Cooke)*

MSC Cruises' *MSC Opera* proceeds away from the City Cruise Terminal in 2012 during her second season on the south coast. The ship was built by Alstom Chantiers de l'Atlantique, Saint-Nazaire, France in 2004 and has a passenger capacity of 2,200. *(Darren Holdaway)*

P&O Cruises' new baby, the 2001 built *Adonia*, passes the *Queen Victoria* and *Grand Princess* on her maiden cruise departure in May 2011. The ship began life as Renaissance Cruises' *R Eight* and then served Swan Hellenic as the *Minerva II* and Princess Cruises as the *Royal Princess*. *(Patricia Dempsey)*

Royal Caribbean's *Vision of the Seas* slips quietly away from Southampton after one of her occasional visits on 29th April 2011. Another product of Chantiers de l'Atlantique, St. Nazaire, France in 1998, she was christened at Southampton on 26th April in that year. *(Andrew Cooke)*

The *Artemis* (ex *Royal Princess*) joined the P&O fleet in 2005 and served with them until April 2011. Built in 1984 for Princess Cruises by Oy Wärtsilä Ab of Helsinki, Finland, she was the largest passenger ship built by the company for the US market in over a decade. *(Andrew Cooke)*

Holland America Line's (HAL) 1997 built *Rotterdam* sails past Hythe on her way into Southampton on the morning of 3rd November 2012 prior to commencing a 32 night Caribbean Odyssey cruise. HAL turnaround cruises from Southampton remain a rarity at this stage. *(John Kennedy)*

This busy May 2012 scene features Silversea Cruises' *Silver Whisper* at Southampton's Queen Elizabeth II Terminal as the Hythe Ferry *Great Expectations* and Red Funnel passenger catamaran *Red Jet 4* pass by on their respective journeys to Town Quay and Cowes. (Andrew Cooke)

Azamara Cruises, part of the Royal Caribbean Group, is one of the less common visitors to the Solent. However, in the summer of 2012 the *Azamara Journey*, built as the *R Six* in 2000, called at Southampton and is shown in the Western Solent approaching the Hurst Narrows. *(Andrew Cooke)*

The *Voyager of the Seas* passes Town Quay, Southampton, in July 2009. Built in 1999 at the Kvaerner Masa Yard in Åbo, Finland, she was the first of four Voyager Class ships built for Royal Caribbean Cruise Lines. Her sister *Adventure of the Seas* will be based here in 2013. *(Kevin Dempsey)*

Currently Europe's largest cruise ship, the *Independence of the Seas* was the third Freedom Class ship built for Royal Caribbean. Here she leaves her homeport and passes Princess Cruises' 1998 built Grand Class ship *Grand Princess* in July 2012 during the latter's final season here. *(Andrew Cooke)*

After inaugural visits by the *Freedom of the Seas* and *Liberty of the Seas* in 2006 and 2007, the third Freedom Class ship *Independence of the Seas* was delivered to Southampton from the shipyard in Finland in April 2008. The gross tonnage of each exceeds 154,000 tonnes. *(Andrew Cooke)*

The top photo depicts the *Independence of the Seas* swinging off Egypt Point, Isle of Wight, whilst sailing for the Mediterranean whereas the above shows the stern view of this floating resort as she passes Hythe on a sunny afternoon in 2012. *(Andrew Cooke)*

The *Oasis of the Seas* became the world's largest cruise ship when completed in 2009, superseding the *Independence of the Seas*. With a gross tonnage of 225,282 grt this stern view was taken as she called at the Solent's Charlie Anchorage in November 2009 (see Page 26) *(Andrew Cooke)*

The second of Celebrity Cruises' Solstice Class ships was the first to visit Southampton. The *Celebrity Equinox* arrived at Southampton upon delivery in July 2009 for her first two cruises. Here she turns into the Eastern Solent off Cowes at the end of her short cruise programme. *(Andrew Cooke)*

The *Celebrity Eclipse* has served Southampton from spring to autumn since her maiden arrival in April 2010 and spends the winter in the Caribbean. Great views at Southampton are possible from aboard a Blue Funnel Cruises' vessel as shown here with the *Celebrity Eclipse* departing. *(Andrew Cooke)*

When the *Grand Princess* was built in 1998 she was the largest passenger ship ever built, with a gross tonnage of 108,806 gross tonnage. The first four Grand Class ships featured the iconic raised Skywalkers Lounge on the stern that was dubbed the "Trolley Handle." *(Andrew Cooke)*

The second series of Grand Class ships commenced with the *Crown Princess* in 2006. She is shown here at Souhampton's Ocean Terminal in 2010, her first season at the port. Also built by Fincantieri at Monfalcone, Italy, these variants lacked the raised "handle" on the stern. *(Andrew Cooke)*

The *Caribbean Princess* heads away from Southampton in the summer of 2012 during her first cruise programme based here, releasing the *Crown Princess* to serve Princess Cruises elsewhere. *(Andrew Cooke)*

One of four sister ships, the *Sea Princess* was delivered from Fincantieri's Monfalcone yard in 1998. In May 2003 she arrived at Southampton as P&O Cruises' *Adonia*, joining her sister *Oceana*. The ship reverted to her former identity at Southampton in 2005 and was later transferred away. *(Andrew Cooke)*

The stern arrangement of the modern cruise ship is often designed for functionality rather than aesthetics. This is demonstrated by the aft view of P&O Cruises' *Ventura* as she sails down Southampton Water behind Cunard Line's *Queen Victoria* in May 2008. *(Andrew Cooke)*

Contrasting passenger vessels! The 2008 built and 3,092 passenger capacity *Ventura* meets the 1992 built and 162 passenger capacity Hythe Ferry *Great Expectations* adjacent to the historic structure of Hythe Pier during May 2012. *(Andrew Cooke)*

A favourite location from where to watch the ships travelling to and from Southampton is Egypt Point, just west of Cowes on the Isle of Wight. Here P&O Cruises' *Ventura* follows the navigation channel from Southampton Water and turns to port to head out to sea via the Eastern Solent. *(Andrew Cooke)*

Another superb location to watch the shipping from is Calshot Spit at the seaward end of Southampton Water. Here the *Azura*, 2010 built near sister to the *Ventura*, approaches this viewpoint from the direction of the port in August 2011. *(Andrew Cooke)*

Viewed from the Hythe Ferry, Norwegian Cruise Line's (NCL) *Norwegian Pearl* sits at the Queen Elizabeth II Terminal in December 2006 during her Media Showcase event. The ship had been delivered the previous month and was the third of four Jewel Class vessels. *(Andrew Cooke)*

In June 2010 NCL introduced its biggest ship to date. The 4,200 passenger capacity *Norwegian Epic* had limped into port on 22nd June due to a propulsion fault but her launch event went ahead and, as shown here, she sailed for New York on a sell-out voyage two days later. *(Andrew Cooke)*

In 2008 NCL's *Norwegian Jade* commenced two seasons operating out of Southampton. She was built by Meyer Werft in Germany and delivered as the *Pride of Hawaii* in 2006. Here the ship departs from the City Cruise Terminal as watched from the new *Eurodam* in June 2008. *(Andrew Cooke)*

NORWEGIAN JADE

NASSAU

Southampton's Ocean Cruise Terminal was opened on 29th May 2009 by ABP Ports at a cost of £19 million, which was funded by Carnival UK for use by their brands including Cunard Line, P&O Cruises and Princess Cruises. The *Ventura* is shown sailing from there in 2011. *(Andrew Cooke)*

Saga Cruises' *Saga Rose* and *Saga Ruby* together at the Queen Elizabeth II Terminal in April 2007. The Saga Rose was built as the *Sagafjord* in 1965, operated by Cunard from 1983-1997 and scrapped in 2010. The *Saga Ruby* was built as the *Vistafjord* (see Page 16). *(Andrew Cooke)*

Saga Cruises' *Saga Ruby* shares Southampton's Western Docks with the *Aurora* on a sunny afternoon. Saga purchased the vessel from Cunard in 2004. Built in 1973 as the *Vistafjord* she became *Caronia* in 1999 and will be retired in 2014 - her 40th season. *(Miles Cowsill)*

The Adsteam tug *Lyndhurst* assists the *Saga Rose* away from the City Cruise Terminal in April 2006 as her younger sister *Saga Ruby* also prepares to leave. Needless to say this occasion produced an abundance of whistle blowing between two grand ladies of cruising. *(Andrew Cooke)*

Launched as Hapag Lloyd's *Europa*, and previously known as the *Bleu de France*, Saga Cruises introduced the 1981 built *Saga Sapphire* in April 2012 replacing the *Saga Pearl II*, which subsequently adopted the name *Quest for Adventure*. Both are shown here at Southampton. *(Patricia Dempsey)*

At around 05.30 on 20th May 2011 P&O Cruises' *Adonia* passed through the Hurst Narrows in the Western Solent, with Hurst Castle as a backdrop. She was on her delivery voyage from the USA having transferred from Princess Cruises whom she served as the *Royal Princess*. *(Andrew Cooke)*

The *Oceana* officially joined the P&O Cruises fleet at Southampton in May 2003 when she was named with her sister *Adonia* by Princess Anne and Zara Phillips. The Fincantieri built ship was delivered in 2000 as the *Ocean Princess* and is shown passing Calshot. *(Andrew Cooke)*

P&O's majestic *Aurora* was built by Meyer Werft as a consort to the *Oriana* and delivered in April 2000. Here the ship is returning to Southampton's Mayflower Cruise Terminal early on the morning of 6th May 2008 as observed from aboard the brand new *Independence of the Seas*. *(John Kennedy)*

The *Oriana* was delivered to P&O Cruises in April 1995. Here she departs from her home port in the summer of 2012 sporting the new 360 tonne ducktail stern that was added during her £25 million refit at Blohm & Voss in Hamburg 16th November- 5th December 2011. *(Andrew Cooke)*

P&O Cruises' 175th Anniversary Grand Event on 3rd July 2012 saw all seven ships in Southampton together. Alas poor weather marred the occasion. Here the *Adonia* leads the *Ventura* away from Western Docks as the *Arcadia, Aurora* and *Oriana* wait to follow in turn. *(P&O Cruises)*

The P&O Grand Event culminated in the ships sailing through the Eastern Solent in two lines, either side of the Trinity House vessel *Patricia*, where they received a Royal Review. Here the Princess Royal greets the *Azura* and *Oceana* with the *Oriana* having already passed by. *(P&O Cruises)*

This photograph rather sums up the summer of 2012. The *Oriana* makes her way around the Thorn Channel on a stormy June afternoon whilst heading away from Southampton for warmer climes. Gurnard Buoy is in the foreground. *(Andrew Cooke)*

The graceful lines of the *Aurora* are shown off very well here in the late afternoon sunshine as she turns off Cowes. The *Aurora* was built by Meyer Werft in Germany as an extended and enhanced version of the *Oriana* and made her service debut in May 2000. *(Andrew Cooke)*

For the first time, two Silversea ships were in a UK port at the same time on 7th September 2011. Later that day the 2001 built *Silver Whisper* leads the 1994 built *Silver Cloud* away from Western Docks, Southampton. Both vessels were built in Italy. *(Patricia Dempsey)*

Portsmouth has played host to several expedition sized cruise ships. One such example is the *National Geographic Explorer* that commenced a cruise from here in May 2012 after refit at Southampton. She was built in 1982 as the *Midnatsol* for Norway's Hurtigruten. *(Andrew Cooke)*

The *Black Prince* is shown de-storing at Southampton after being retired by Fred Olsen Cruise Lines (FOCL) on 16th October 2009. She was built as a dual purpose ship in 1966, converted for full-time cruising in 1987; she was sold to Venezuelan interests in November 2009 as the *Ola Smeralda*. *(Andrew Cooke)*

Fred. Olsen Cruises' *Black Watch* prepares to sail from Southampton in 2009. This popular ship was built in 1972 by Oy Wärtsilä Ab, Helsinki, Finland as the *Royal Viking Star*. Fred. Olsen purchased the 880 passenger capacity vessel in 1996. *(Andrew Cooke)*

This 2009 view features Fred. Olsen Cruises' 804 passenger capacity *Boudicca* at Berth 38/39 in Southampton. The vessel was constructed as the *Royal Viking Sky* in 1973 and sold to Fred. Olsen Cruises in 2005 when she acquired the eighth name of her career. *(Andrew Cooke)*

The *Balmoral* entered service for Fred. Olsen Cruises in 2008 as their largest vessel and was photographed here sailing away from Southampton in August 2012. Four months earlier she had operated a special Titanic Memorial Cruise from here. *(Darren Holdaway)*

The *Grand Princess* prepares to sail from Southampton during her final season here in 2012. Note the absence of her "Trolley Handle" at the stern on Deck 18. This was removed during a refit at Freeport's Grand Bahama Shipyard 11th April-4th May 2011. The *Ventura* completes the scene. *(Andrew Cooke)*

In June 2008 Holland America Line's Signature Class ship *Eurodam* was shown off to UK travel agents and media at Southampton's berth 104. Here she is passing the beach at Calshot after the event. The *Eurodam* was built at Fincantieri's Porto Maghera Yard in Italy. *(Andrew Cooke)*

In April 2008 Cunard Line assembled the QM2, QE2 (final refit) and *Queen Victoria* together at Southampton for the first time. Also in port that day was Princess Cruises' *Pacific Princess* that began life as the *R Three* for Renaissance Cruises in 1999 and was purchased in 2002. *(Andrew Cooke)*

The *Artemis* left the P&O fleet in 2011 having been sold to Artania Shipping of Bermuda in November 2009 and chartered back to P&O. The ship was renamed *Artania*, chartered to German operator Phoenix Reisen in May 2011 and returned to her old stomping ground in July 2011. *(Andrew Cooke)*

The *Sundream* was a regular at Southampton 2000-2004 and is captured in the evening sun at the City Cruise Terminal in June 2004, her final season with MyTravel. She was built in 1970 at Helsinki for Royal Caribbean Cruises as the *Song of Norway* and sold as a Casino in 2012. *(Andrew Cooke)*

On 26th February 2010 MSC Cruises brought their latest ship to Southampton direct from her builders, STX Europe in St. Nazaire, France. The fourth Musica Class ship, the *MSC Magnifica* was later christened in Hamburg on 6th March 2010. *(Andrew Cooke)*

Delivered to French operator Compagnie du Ponant Yacht Cruises in May 2010, the brand new luxury cruise vessel *Le Boreal* sails through the Hurst Narrows in the Western Solent on a sunny 26th June 2010 en route to Southampton on her maiden call. *(Andrew Cooke)*

The *Ocean Village Two* departs from Southampton in April 2007 on her maiden voyage for the Ocean Village brand, followed by the *Constellation*. Named at what is now Ocean Terminal, she was delivered to P&O Princess Cruises in 1990 as the *Crown Princess* and is now *Pacific Jewel*. *(Andrew Cooke)*

All records were broken on 29th April 2006 when Royal Caribbean's giant *Freedom of the Seas* arrived at Southampton having been delivered five days earlier. Here she heads away on her transatlantic voyage to New York/Miami, followed by Red Funnel's vehicle ferry *Red Osprey*. *(Andrew Cooke)*

Phoenix Reisen's *Amadea* clearly shows her Japanese heritage in this view at Southampton in July 2006. She was delivered to Nippon Yusen Kaisha, Tokyo, Japan, in December 1991 as the *Asuka* and is chartered to Phoenix Reisen from Amadea Shipping Co. Ltd., Bahamas. *(Andrew Cooke)*

Different eras of cruising: The traditional 1972 built cruise ship *Black Watch* follows the 2008 built "floating resort" *Independence of the Seas* and the 21st Century Liner *Queen Mary 2* down Southampton Water outbound. Red Funnel's *Red Jet 4* completes the scene. *(Andrew Cooke)*

With the shore defences of Calshot Castle in the foreground, P&O Cruises' *Azura* traverses Southampton water a fairly quiet afternoon. The 2010 built *Azura* is easily identifiable by her duck-tail stern which does not feature on the *Ventura*. *(Andrew Cooke)*

The job of maintaining a cruise ship is never ending. Here P&O Cruises' 2005 built *Arcadia*, a member of Fincantieri's ubiquitous family of Vista Class ships, receives attention to paintwork around her bow and anchor whilst at the Ocean Terminal, which opened in May 2009. *(Darren Holdaway)*

With much whistle blowing the *Oceana* passes the Queen Elizabeth II Cruise Terminal having sailed away from the nearby Ocean Terminal. She is passed by Red Funnel Ferries' 1998 built *Red Jet 3* nearing the end of her journey between Cowes, Isle of Wight, and Town Quay. *(Andrew Cooke)*

This April 2005 aerial view shows Cunard Line's 2003 built *Queen Mary 2* proceeding through Southampton Docks and passing the 1969 built *Queen Elizabeth 2* at Berth 38/39. Above the QM2 is Ocean Dock is where the *Titanic* sailed from and the Ocean Terminal was built. *(Southern Echo)*

The *Queen Mary 2* arrived at her homeport from Chantiers de l'Atlantique, St. Nazaire, on Boxing Day in 2003 and continues as the only transatlantic cruise liner in operation. Here she waits at Berth 38/39 prior to sailing to New York once again during Summer 2012. *(Darren Holdaway)*

The QE2 sailed from Southampton for the final time bound for Dubai on 11th November 2008 and has been sadly missed. Here the ever-popular transatlantic icon leaves the Queen Elizabeth II Terminal (Berth 38/39) on a cruise in the twilight of her 39 year career. *(Miles Cowsill)*

Two of Cunard Line's three Queens are Vista Class vessels produced by Italian shipbuilder Fincantieri. Here the 2010 built *Queen Elizabeth* is shadowed by Hythe Ferry *Great Expectations*. The Cunard ships were controversially re-registered in Hamilton from late 2011. *(Andrew Cooke)*

Cunard Line's three ships were in Southampton together twice in 2012. The second event was 13th July and here the *Queen Elizabeth* leads the *Queen Victoria* and *Queen Mary 2* out of Southampton Water as viewed from the pursuing Blue Funnel Cruises vessel. *(Darren Holdaway)*

The *Queen Mary 2* arrives back home at first light on 5th June 2012, followed by the *Queen Victoria* and *Queen Elizabeth*, to celebrate the Diamond Jubilee of Her Majesty Queen Elizabeth II. Southampton tug *Svitzer Sarah* provided a suitable welcome to each ship in turn. *(Andrew Cooke)*

A new era for Cunard. The brand new *Queen Victoria* rests at Southampton's City Cruise Terminal on the morning of 7th December 2007 having just completed her delivery voyage from Fincantieri's Porto Marghera yard in Italy. The local refuse vessel is seen alongside. *(Andrew Cooke)*

On 8th January 2008 the new *Queen Victoria* prepares to sail from the City Cruise Terminal on her maiden transatlantic voyage in tandem with the grand old lady of the fleet, the QE2. The new ship lead the duo away from port after a firework display off Mayflower Park. *(Andrew Cooke)*

The third P&O ship to be named *Arcadia* (built 1989 and formerly the *Star Princess*) arrived in 1997 from Princess Cruises. In this March 1999 view she is passing Hythe Pier with a Red Funnel car ferry for company. In 2003 she became the *Ocean Village* and *Pacific Pearl* in 2010. *(Andrew Cooke)*

Celebrity Cruises' *Mercury* was the third and final Century Class vessel and was delivered in 1997 by Meyer Werft, Papenburg, Germany. She called at the Queen Elizabeth II Cruise Terminal when brand new and transferred from Celebrity to TUI Cruises as the *Mein Schiff 2* in 2011. *(Andrew Cooke)*

In June 1994 the *Seabourn Pride* visited the Solent to take part in the D-Day 50th Anniversary Fleet Review and is seen here at anchor. The ship was delivered to Seabourn Cruise Line by Schichau-Seebeckwerft, Bremerhaven in November 1988. *(Andrew Cooke)*

The *Disney Wonder* was the second vessel added to the Disney Cruise Line fleet in 1999 having been constructed by the Fincantieri Marghera Shipyard at Breda, Italy. She called at Southampton's Berth 38/39 in July 1999 on her delivery voyage to Port Canaveral, USA. *(Andrew Cooke)*

Costa Cruises' ships are not regular visitors to Southampton but this view shows the *Costa Classica* at Berth 38/39 in August 1993. Another product of a Fincantieri shipyard, the 1,766 passenger capacity vessel had been delivered two years earlier. *(Andrew Cooke)*

On 13th October 2012 Southampton hosted another first when two Celebrity Cruises ships were in port together. Here the 2010 built *Celebrity Eclipse* is shown outward bound for Ponta Delgada whilst the 2002 built *Celebrity Constellation* prepares to sail for Le Havre. *(Andrew Cooke)*

The Hurtigruten Coastal Cruise vessel *Nordnorge* paid a visit to Portsmouth circa 2003 and here she heads towards The Needles past Sconce Point, west of Yarmouth, in the Western Solent at sunset. The ship was built in 1997 by Kvaerner Kleven of Ulsteinvik in Norway. *(Andrew Cooke)*

Hapag Lloyd Cruises' *c.Columbus* prepares to sail after a call at Cowes, Isle of Wight, during the summer of 2011. Built by MTW Schiffswerft, Wismar, Germany in 1997 she was chartered to Plantours & Partner in 2012 and renamed *Hamburg*. *(Andrew Cooke)*

The *Island Sky* regularly visits the anchorage off Cowes as on this occasion in August 2011. Built as the *Renaissance Eight* in 1992 she was sold in 2001 after Renaissance Cruises ceased trading. Renamed *Island Sky* in 2004, she has operated for London's Noble Caledonia from 2010. *(Andrew Cooke)*

The *Vistamar* in Cowes Roads off the town of Cowes. In the background can be seen Portsmouth's Spinnaker Tower. The ship dates from 1989 and was operated by Plantours until 2012 when she passed to Lebanese Abou Merhi Cruises and became the *Orient Queen II*. *(Andrew Cooke)*

One of the most attractive looking small cruise ships is Hapag Lloyd's *Europa*. Another regular at the three Solent cruise ports, the vessel is shown during a call at Cowes in the summer of 2011. The ship was built in 1999 by Kværner Masa Yards, Helsinki, Finland. *(Andrew Cooke)*

An aerial view of Portsmouth International Port showing the new 2,700m² terminal building to the right of the photo, which opened on 1st April 2011 as part of a £16.5 million upgrade. The *Discovery* occupies Ro-Ro berth 2 with Brittany Ferries' *Mont St. Michel* at berth 4. *(Portsmouth Int. Port)*

The *Athena* departing Portsmouth in April 2011 for refit having completed a voyage that had commenced in Australia several weeks earlier. This cruising veteran was built in 1948 as the *Stockhom* for Swedish American Line. Several identities later she became the *Athena* in 2005. *(Andrew Cooke)*

The *Hebridean Princess* passes Sconce Buoy off Fort Victoria having sailed through the Hurst Narows on a gentle amble between Poole and Portsmouth in August 2011. This popular ship began life as David MacBrayne's Ltd ferry *Columba* in 1964 and was sold/converted for cruising in 1989. *(Andrew Cooke)*

The *Delphin Voyager* is shown visiting Portsmouth during the 2010 season. Built in Tokyo in 1990 as the *Orient Venus* she passed to Dolphin Cruises Ltd (Germany) in 2007 who filed for bankruptcy in October 2010. During 2012 she was renamed *Aegean Paradise*, her sixth identity. *(Andrew Cooke)*

A Classic Beauty. The 1971 built *Discovery* departs from Portsmouth in July 2012 operating for Voyages of Discovery as she had since 2003. The vessel was built as the *Island Venture* prior to charter/sale to Princess Cruises/P&O as the *Island Princess*. Last renamed in 2002. *(Andrew Cooke)*

In May 2012 the *Marco Polo* debuted at Portsmouth International Port. Built in 1965 by Mathias-Thesen Werft, East Germany as the *Aleksandr Pushkin* for the Soviet Union's Baltic Shipping Company, she became *Marco Polo* in 1993 and is shown leaving Portsmouth. *(Andrew Cooke)*

The ships of Hurtigruten are not confined to the Norwegian Coastal Services and here the *Fram* is shown at Portsmouth on 30th September 2011. Built in 2007 by Fincantieri in Trieste, Italy, the vessel was on a Round Britain cruise from Hamburg with 230 passengers aboard. *(Portsmouth Int. Port)*

The small 122 passenger capacity expedition cruise ship *Clipper Adventurer* is shown here on the Bar Channel having sailed out of Portsmouth Harbour in 2004. The ice strengthened vessel is the sister ship to the *Lyubov Orlova* and was built in 1975 as the *Alla Tarasova*. *(Andrew Cooke)*

The *Expediton*, depicted here leaving Portsmouth after her second visit in May 2010, began life as the vehicle ferry *Kattegat* in 1972. She then became the Dover based *Tiger* for P&O Normandy Ferries and Townsend Thoresen before serving Viking Line as the *Alandsfarjan* until 2007. *(Andrew Cooke)*

P&O Cruises' *Arcadia* swings to the east off Egypt Point, located between Gurnard and Cowes, whilst negotiating the Thorn Channel that links Southampton Water and the Solent. Closer to shore a traditional yacht saunters by whilst returning to the sailing mecca of Cowes. *(Andrew Cooke)*

Acknowledgements

My thanks go to the following for their assistance with this book: Beth Evans, Lorraine Nottley & Doug Morrison (ABP Southampton), Blue Funnel Cruises (Southampton), John Hendy, William Mayes, Chris Bancroft, Darren Holdaway, Dr. Allan Ryszka-Onions, Fotoflite, John & Rozanne Kennedy, Julie Blackwell (Navigate Design PR - Portsmouth International Port), Kerry Jackson (Wightlink Isle of Wight Ferries), Michael Gallagher (Cunard Line), Nigel Lawrence, P&O Cruises, Patricia Dempsey, Rod Hodson (Deputy Harbour Master, Cowes), Sue Hill (Collections Access Officer - Southampton City Council), Solent & Wightline Cruises (Cowes) and the Southern Echo.

This book is dedicated to my wife, Donna, my Mother and Father and to my late Grandad, Francis "Bob" Frise, as they have always fully supported and encouraged my love of ships and the sea.